DÉJEUNERS,
GOÛTERS,
COLLATIONS,
BRUNCHES.
EURYDICE
10, Place des Vosges
75004 Paris
Tél. : 42.77.77.99
№ 000242

Notes from PARIS:

A Tale of Two Friends in the City of Light

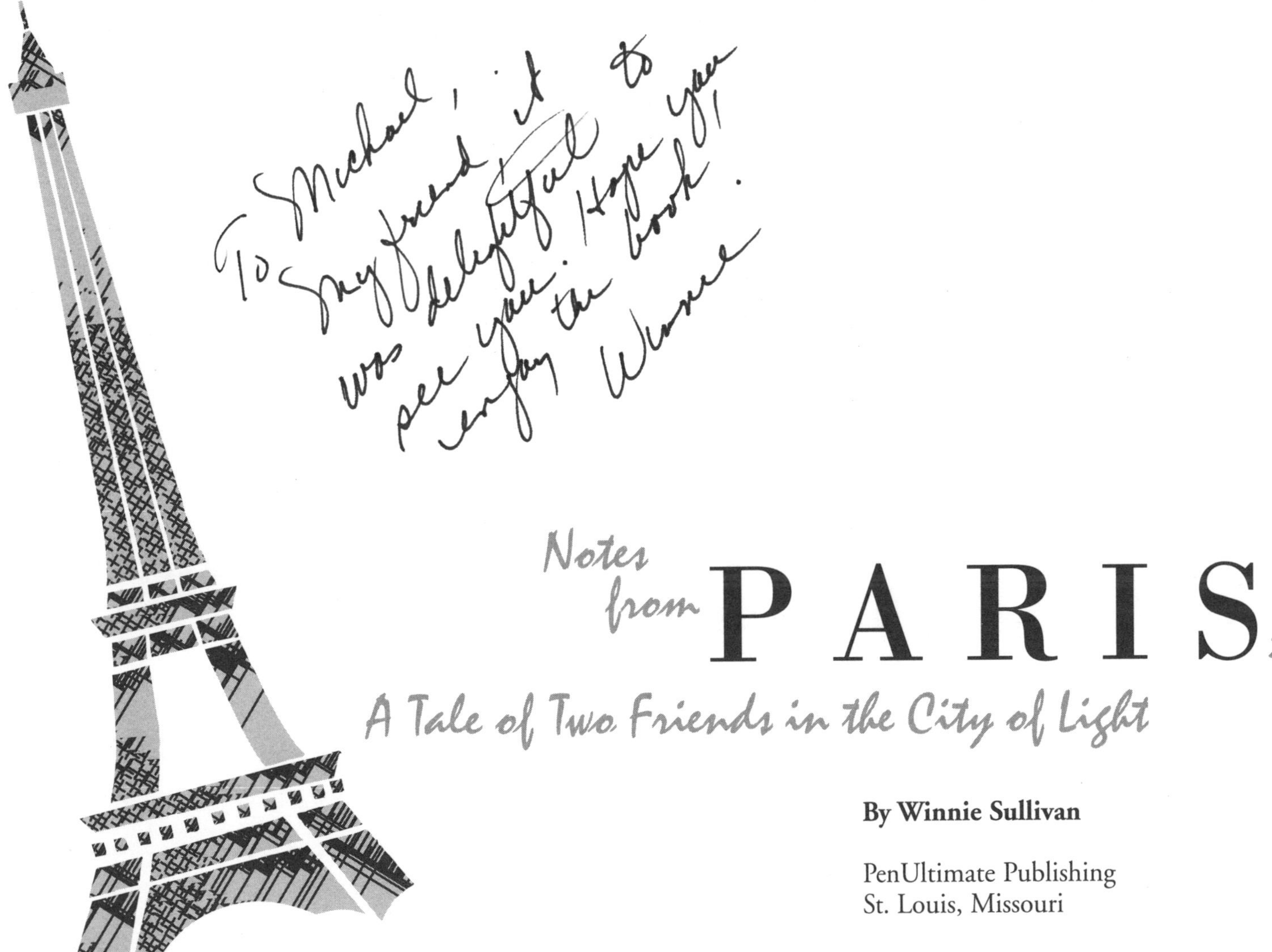

Notes from

PARIS:

A Tale of Two Friends in the City of Light

By Winnie Sullivan

PenUltimate Publishing
St. Louis, Missouri

Publisher: PenUltimate Publishing
Design/Production: 5 twenty nine design
Cover, Interior and Polaroid Illustrations: Joanne Kluba
Printer: BookMasters, Inc.

© 2003, by PenUltimate Publishing
606 North and South Road,
St. Louis, Missouri   63130
Phone: (314) 862-3842   Fax: (314) 862-5911
E-mail: penultim@swbell.net   Website: www.penultimatepbl.com

Library of Congress Control Number: 2002105803

Sullivan, Winnie, 1950-
Notes from Paris: a tale of two friends in the city of light/Winnie Sullivan
p.   cm.
ISBN   0-615-12100-4
1. Travel   2. Paris (France)-Description and travel

Printed in the United States of America

Printing 10 9 8 7 6 5 4 3 2

without
whom nothing would be
possible.

Mme. Anne Nakas, who
gave me the words with
which to share her
culture
and
Sr. Rosalie, who handed
me the pen to describe
the experience.

Dedication

I extend
a special thanks
to,

the following individuals, each of
whom made a unique contribution
to the book: to Maria Sanderson, for
creating and effecting a design and
art program that, quite beyond mere-
ly complementing the text, took on a
life of its own; to Joanne Kluba,
whose beautiful illustrations so accu-
rately capture the emotional content
of these journal notes; to Alan
Boime, Patricia Cagle, Lynn
Rosemann, and Charles and
Jacqueline Williams, who shared
with me their photographs from
Paris; and to Leslie Rickard, Judith
Roos and Susan Wright, whose
efforts and advice regarding produc-
tion of the book I value greatly.

Acknowledgments

Notes from
PARIS:

A Tale of

Two Friends

in the

City of Light

Table of Contents

I don't know how the seed of Paris got planted in my soul—a bookish, black wisp of a girl from Chicago's South Side—but it's always been there, taking root in me as I grew to recognize it. By the age of seven or eight, I loved the *Madeline* books. By the time I was eleven, I knew I would study French. The stories of African-Americans in Paris—Baker, Baldwin, Wright—only fanned the flame. As I turned sixteen, immersed in the language, I realized I'd have to visit Paris, and I understood, in advance, that I'd feel at home when I did.

About twenty-five years later, that chance arrived. To preserve the memory in a way that photographs alone cannot, I kept a journal while there. On the occasion of my friend, coworker, and traveling buddy Robin's move from St. Louis to Boston, I transcribed the journal to give to her as a going-away present. Now, those journal notes have formed this book.

Robin and I became friends at work. In the midst of a career transition from the social services to

writing and editing, I thought I'd enjoy sampling—as an older student intern—the field of health science publishing. Robin, the internship supervisor, facilitated my eventual employment at the publishing company. As time wore on, we discovered that we shared—as might be expected of many who work in the world of publishing—a love of literature; beyond that, we're both Francophiles. Thus, one of our first joint activities was to become founding members of a book club, which ambitiously set out to read—as its initial selection—Marcel Proust's *Remembrance of Things Past*.

Finally, we decided to plan a trip to Paris. Robin had been there before, although as part of a more extensive trip abroad. This would be my first visit. We bought tons of travel guides and took courses to refresh our French. While we were planning the trip, I don't think that we had any idea how well-suited we would be as traveling companions. Neither of us is an avid shopper, so there was a clear, though unspo-

Introduction

ken, agreement that the Paris fashion scene and department stores would not be a focus of our trip. We each have a streak of adventurousness and so were content to do a lot of walking—sometimes off the beaten path—and, generally, to achieve a balance between seeing the mandatory sights and experiencing something of day-to-day life in the short time we would be there. As a result, this is not a tour guide. It does not point out the *right* places to visit in Paris. It is my first person, active voice invitation to experience the joy of travel; to stand in unsophisticated, gaping awe before sights one could only dream about; and to appreciate how friendship multiplies the fun.

As I've gone back to prepare these notes for publication, I know I've probably imposed a somewhat reflective tone on what had been a more humorous account of our adventure. I'm aware of all that has changed during the ten years since our trip, although as the French would say *plus ça change, plus ç'est la meme chose*—the more things change, the more they remain the same. I'm yet in St. Louis; Robin lives in Arizona. I've not made a second trip to Paris, though each year holds that promise… there are so many more "Parises" to see. Here is the cherished memory of one of them. Enjoy!

Winnie Sullivan

April 23

Departure from Saint Louis - 3:45 P.M., Flight 818

Mom's blowing. She's on time, as usual, and I can hear her impatience in the horn. I asked her to go with me—actually, to take me to the airport. Artie's coming to see me off, too, and we're all a little uneasy, knowing that I'll be away from home—far away from home—for almost two weeks. I'm excited but anxious; I hate to fly. Robin doesn't like flying, but she's not quite as bad as I am.

At the airport, we spot Robin and Michael. Robin and I check our bags and we all head for the gate. We have a few minutes before it's time for us to board and, as we wait, we gaze through the window at the big 767 on which we'll soon be departing.

Goodbyes said, we're on the plane, taxiing, lifting ... months of planning (and a lifetime of dreaming) nearing realization. Trying to calm myself, I look around at the other passengers. They're settling in, getting comfortable, arranging carry-ons and pil-lows, quieting toddlers, talking to the person in the adjoining seat, picking up where they've left off in a favorite book. I'm tempted to call out, "Is anyone else going to Paris for the first time?"

We hear the pilot on the PA apologizing to passengers who were inconvenienced last night. Robin and I wonder what he's talking about, but instead of asking, we decide to refine a few plans. Though neither of us is a "tour type," we've been considering a walking tour that includes the Père Lachaise cemetery, the haunts of Hemingway, and the historic landmarks on the Left Bank. Probably, we'll opt for the adventure of exploring these sites on our own.

The flight is long, tiring. I'm counting the hours but, after a couple of glasses of wine, I'm no longer clutching the armrest. Overall it's been a smooth flight, no turbulence. We have dinner en route and, later, breakfast.

> **I'm counting the hours but, after a couple of glasses of wine, I'm no longer clutching the armrest.**

Departure from St. Louis

The Roissy-Charles de Gaulle Airport is one of two main air travel facilities in the Paris metropolitan area. Located 16 miles northeast of the city, Roissy-CDG consists of three passenger terminal complexes which, in the year 2000, served approximately 48 million passengers.* The airport is also a major freight and postal hub.

The Roissy-CDG Airport came into service in 1974. Despite its very modern appearance, the airport rests on a site that's rich with its own history. The area of Roissy-CDG actually covers all or part of six villages: Roissy, Mesnil-Amelot, Mauregard, Tremblay, Epiais les Louvres, and Mitry-Mory. In centuries past these boroughs were home to vineyards, an ancient windmill, and an old coaching inn frequented by straw merchants. They were the scenes of trysts—on the Lovers' Pathway—and, reportedly, incorporate routes traveled by the ancient Gauls, as well as by Louis XVI as he sought to escape Paris for safe haven in Lorraine.

*Source: 2002 Annual Report, Aeroports of Paris

The Roissy–Charles de Gaulle Airport
Image by Werner Krutein/photovault.com

April 24

**Arrival at Roissy-Charles de Gaulle,
Getting Acquainted**

We're almost there. The pilot calls our attention to the North Atlantic below as it pounds the western coast of France. Now we're descending into . . . FOG. We are socked in. Two things I'm glad I didn't know about in advance—the fog and the fact that the plane had had a mechanical problem the night before we left. Apparently, after about three hours into the flight, they'd had to circle back to Saint Louis—the airline's hub. Had I known that, I'd have been checking into steamboat passage or maybe trans-Atlantic hovercraft (*do they have those?*).

After landing we follow the airport maze to the baggage claim. The signage is French, the loudspeaker announcements are French—yep, we're really here. Roissy reminds me of a movie set for a low-budget futuristic film; people, with their luggage, ride along on conveyors in suspended, transparent tubes.

I'm apprehensive about Customs because my suitcase is bulging, . . .

Observing this strange scene, I remember that we're about to pass through Customs. I'm apprehensive about Customs because my suitcase is bulging, and I'm afraid I'm going to have to ask the Customs agent to sit on it so that I can close it again. But what Customs? They stamp our *fiche de débarquement* (landing pass) but don't even look *at* our suitcases, let alone *in* them.

We spot a restroom and decide to make a brief stop, the first in a series of French bathroom "experiences." We take little note, at first, that men and women are entering through the same door. Inside, we become aware that the men's and women's restrooms are separated by a short partition, around which one can quite easily see. OK, this *is* different. Some of the English and American women behind us in line acknowledge the difference a little more vocally.

Next, we're off to the train station by *navette*, i.e., the shuttle. We want to get a *carnet*—a weeklong transit pass—but decide, for now, to buy one *billet*—a one-way ticket for the commuter train to Paris, the

Standing on the Place du Châtelet, one has little awareness of the magnitude of its subterranean activity—a convergence of rail lines making it the crossroads of Paris— nor can one easily imagine the goings-on that marked the history of this site. Formerly, the Grand Châtelet fortress, built in the twelfth century by Louis IV to control access to the Right Bank, stood at this location. After construction of the enclosure of Philippe-Auguste, the Châtelet was no longer the first line of defense on the Right Bank and became, instead, the headquarters of the provost of Paris. Here suspects were tried, convicted, imprisoned and tortured; some were taken to the Place de Grève, now the Place de l'Hôtel de Ville, for public execution. The Grand Châtelet was demolished in 1802.

Today, on the west side of the Place du Châtelet, sits the Theatre du Châtelet—now known as the Theatre Musicale de Paris. Across the square to the east is the Theatre de la Ville, the old Sarah Bernhardt Theater. In the middle of the square is the Fontaine du Palmier (the Palm Fountain), built in 1808 in honor of Napoleon's triumphant Egyptian campaign.

The Place du Châtelet

Réseau Express Régional, or RER. It's a nice ride into the city, lasting about a half hour, but Robin and I are surprised by the amount of graffiti defacing the stone wall along the rail track.

The train arrives at the Châtelet station. After walking through a seemingly endless maze of more tubes from the RER, with Parisians surreally whizzing by, Robin and I emerge into the square named for the former Grand Châtelet fortress and prison and begin the trek to our hotel, which is on the Ile Saint-Louis. We lug our suitcases along the Quai Hôtel de Ville to the Pont Louis-Phillippe to cross the Seine. Robin's bag (on wheels) isn't working properly and keeps tilting over. Having been awake now for a day and a half, we find the dysfunctional suitcase inexplicably hilarious. We're laughing and having to stop every few steps to set the bag upright—a strange sight, no doubt, to passers-by.

Robin and I have been rewarded for pouring over countless tour books. We find that the Ile Saint-Louis—right in the middle of the Seine—is a great choice. We're positioned perfectly to tour, on any given day, either the Right or the Left Bank and, if we're feeling particularly ambitious, both. Our hotel is nestled in among other seventeenth-century townhouses. I smile at the thought of telling a yet-to-be-made acquaintance in Paris that Robin and I are from Saint Louis, staying at the Hôtel Saint-Louis, in the Rue Saint-Louis en l'Ile, on the Ile Saint-Louis.

At the reception desk, a man who looks Middle Eastern greets us. He speaks some English and tells us that our room isn't ready yet. It won't be ready until noon—in about two hours. He directs us to put our luggage in a corner of the reception area and tells us to go downstairs to the restaurant, if we want breakfast. We go down spiral steps to a lovely little cavern with tables and chairs and small arched windows. We order café au lait and croissants *avec de la confiture* (with jam)—delicious, but pricey (42F for each of us). The warmth of the coffee helps us to

We're laughing and having to stop every few steps to set the bag upright . . .

. . . lovely little cavern

The Ile Saint-Louis, adjacent to the Ile de la Cité, is the smaller of the two islands that lie in the middle of the Seine River. Named after Louis IX, Saint-Louis, this tract of land was, itself, formed during the seventeenth century from the union of two islets—the Isle aux Vaches (Island of the Cows) and the Isle Notre Dame. Afterwards, the Ile Saint-Louis became the chosen address of nobility, poets, artists and philosophers, government officials, and financiers whose stately mansions hover protectively over the narrow, tree-lined streets. Though linked to the Right and Left Banks and to the Ile de la Cité by numerous bridges, the Ile Saint-Louis provides a peaceful respite from the liveliness of the city.

The Ile Saint-Louis

The Ile de la Cité is the *heart* of Paris. In centuries past, it was the *whole* of Paris. Located in the middle of the Seine River—an appropriate spot for a boat-shaped parcel of land—the Ile de la Cité was settled by a tribe of Celtic Gauls toward the end of the third century B.C. It was this tribe—the Parisii—that lent its name to the city of Paris.

Despite the natural defense provided by the river, inhabitants of the Ile de la Cité—marshalled by the Gallic leader, Vercingétorix—were overtaken by the Romans in A.D. 52 , during the reign of Julius Caesar. Under Roman rule, the island settlement—then known as Lutetia Parisiorum—was extended to the Left Bank. In the fifth century A.D., Clovis, leader of the Franks, united Gaul, defeated the Romans, and made Paris the capital of the new kingdom.

During the Middle Ages, the Ile de la Cité remained the locus of religious and governmental power—the font from which events rippled outward to affect the whole of France. Evidence of the island's centrality in the lives of the people are its structures dating from medieval times: Notre Dame Cathedral, the Sainte-Chapelle, and the Conciergerie.

The Ile de la Cité was dramatically altered in its appearance and population at the hands of Baron Georges Haussman—prefect under Napoleon III—who demolished residences, enlarged streets, and constructed new edifices, among them the Prefecture of Police and the Palais de Justice (law courts).

Today the island still hums with activity—from the law officials setting about their daily course of administrative duties to the eager tourists queuing up to view the landmarks. The Place Dauphine at the western tip of the island and the Square Jean XXIII to the east offer some escape from the bustle . . . a quiet moment to slip through a portal of time where the centuries fall away.

Notre Dame Cathedral on the Ile de la Cité

relax as we try to take in out new surroundings.

Being the last to leave the restaurant, we decide to go out for a walk. We head in the direction of the Ile de la Cité and—more quickly than we expect—are standing before the eastern facade of the Cathedral of Notre Dame de Paris. I blink and have to stop for a moment to convince myself that this is not an illusion. We cross the Pont Saint-Louis, move toward a park bench, flop down, and gaze up at the flying buttresses.

Tourists are everywhere, amid rows and rows of tour buses. We learn that, in fact, we're sitting in the Square Jean XXIII with its flowers—tulips the color of sunlit bordeaux. We walk around the exterior of Notre Dame along the south front and view one of the cathedral's three rose windows. Then on to the west to see the portals, and to stand in the *parvis*—the square in front of Notre Dame from which all distances in France are measured. The day, which started out overcast, has begun to clear and we sit watching tourists

feed the pigeons. The church is asymmetrical, we notice, and pollution has taken its toll on the facade, although restoration is underway.

We head back to the Ile Saint-Louis along its southern quai and are interested to learn, en route, how French parking meters—*horodateurs* or *parcmètres*—work. Then, continuing our walk around the island, we find an *épicerie* (grocer) and get a newspaper—the *International Herald Tribune*—at a kiosque.

Back at the hotel, our room is ready. We can take the winding stairway up to the third floor, or the elevator. We choose the latter. Our room is *très petite*—very small. We have two single beds, a dresser, two nightstands with lamps, a radio, no television; but a clean, private bathroom and toilet—*une salle de bain et W.C.*—and that's all we need.

We start to claim the space, putting some of our clothing and personal items away and hoping that we've struck a balance between packing light and being prepared, armed as we are with miniature sewing kits, electrical adaptors, and other various and sundry "necessities." So far, we've followed family and friends' traveling advice for countering jet lag (drink lots of water; after you arrive, try to stay awake until night). But I'm sitting on my bed and—knowing I can't resist it much longer—lie down for a bit. Robin fights the sleep witch by heading out for another walk.

I awake ready to cram as many activities as possible into the rest of the day. We make plans for the afternoon: buy a *télécarte*—a prepaid phone card; make a call home from the post office; and see some more sights until dinner.

We turn again toward the Ile de la Cité and stroll around the Palais de Justice (the law courts), near the Sainte-Chapelle, through the flower market, and along the Quai de l'Horloge, past the clock tower of the Conciergerie. Then on to the Left Bank, by which time we are starving. We soon discover that French restaurants are not open throughout the day. Most are open for lunch, and then again for dinner, which isn't served until 7:00 or 8:00 P.M.

We turn to our guide books for some ideas and find Le Muniche, a restaurant that opens for dinner at 6:00 P.M. We're off, down the Rue Dauphine to the Rue de Buci. These are narrow, twisting streets with little room for walking on the sidewalks. Marvelous sights: beautiful buildings, tall and narrow, with elaborate, laced iron balconies; outdoor markets. We get to Le Muniche—it has moved. By this time we're ravenous. We spot a café called Le Dauphin and head in. Robin asks for onion soup—*soupe l'oignon gratinée*—and I have *jambon de pays* (a ham sandwich) on a baguette.

After dinner, back to the hotel, where we plan for the next few days and try to begin grasping the value and recognizing the appearance of French money. We're sound asleep by 8:00 P.M.

Then on to the Left Bank, by which time we are starving.

...on a baguette.

The Tour Saint-Jacques

Built between 1508 and 1522, the Tour St. Jacques—flamboyantly Gothic in its architectural style—is a tower without a church. Formerly, it was the bell tower of the Church of St. Jacques, the headquarters of the butchers' guild, that served as the gathering spot for pilgrims on the road south to Santiago de Compostella in Spain, said to be the location of the tomb of St. James the Apostle. The Church of St. Jacques was destroyed in 1802. The statue of the French mathematician and philosopher, Blaise Pascal, stands at the base of tower commemorating the scientific experiments he performed there. The Tour St. Jacques is now used as a meteorological station.

The hands of the clock on the bell tower of Saint-Germain-des-Prés have a wide sweep. They trace an arc that originates with the sixth-century founding of the abbey, traverses the monastery's ascendancy in the Middle Ages and its demise as a victim of the Revolution, and rounds into the emergence of the artistic and literary vibrancy for which the quarter that bears the abbey's remnants is now known.

The Benedictine abbey of Saint-Germain-des-Prés, located on the left bank of the Seine, was built at the direction of Childebert I—son of Clovis—who ordered its construction to house relics seized from the Vandals. It was named after Saint Germanus, the bishop of Paris during the sixth century.

Despite having been ravaged many times during the Norman invasions of the tenth century, the abbey was—by the Middle Ages—a thriving center of scholarship whose holdings extended as far west as the Champs de Mars. The anticlerical fervor of the Revolution brought an end to the monastery's prominence, however; many of its properties were seized or destroyed and, in September, 1793, hundreds of priests and monks were massacred.

Today only the church and the abbot's palace remain. While in the neighboring cafés, the air is charged with the brilliance of past patrons—Sartre, de Beauvoir, Wright, Ingres, Hemingway, Delacroix—whose words and images, like tiny filaments, set the City of Light aglow.

April 25

From Left to Right

We've slept about thirteen hours. *Incroyable!* But, once awake, we're ready to go. We head toward the Châtelet metro to buy a *carnet*, stopping on the way for café au lait at a coffee shop named for the French actress, Sarah Bernhardt (1844-1923). The "Divine Sarah" had performed at a nearby theater. I order *une tartine de beurre* (a slice of bread and butter) and get—another baguette. And I don't even like bread that much! But the French, despite the diminishing number of bakeries, continue their love affair with bread. They walk down the street munching their baguettes, whose long, uneven ends—like a set of leavened bagpipes—refuse to be concealed in grocery sacs.

Watching people from the window of the café, Robin and I muse about the French style. I notice the clothing . . . classic but not conformist, with individualizing touches—a scarf carefully flung, a colorful hat, a jeweled accessory—that lend flair and evoke the word *panache*. As I become aware that many of the passers-by have dark coloring—dark hair, an almost olive skin color, and sharp features—I recall the many cultural influences reflected in the appearance, language, and manner of the French. And of course, people from around the world continue to be drawn here.

It's raining a little. We leave the café and cross to the north corner of the Place du Châtelet to get a closer look at the Tour Saint-Jacques, which is all that remains of Saint-Jacques-la-Boucherie—the parish church of the butchers' guild—that was demolished during the Revolution. We head toward the metro where we purchase our *carnet* and start walking, intending to save the metro tickets to use when we get tired.

From the Place Saint-Michel, past the fountain, we turn into the Rue Saint-André des Arts. Again, little specialty shops everywhere—bookstores, antique dealers, stationery shops. Into the Rue de Buci to the Boulevard Saint-Germain. We come to Saint-Germain-des-Prés. The church—part of the former Benedictine

And I don't even like bread that much!

abbey—marks the site on which a religious institution has stood for fifteen centuries. Inside, the church is very somber. Forbidding confessionals and, of course, chairs, no pews. It has a gigantic organ in the rear. The bell tower of Saint-Germain-des-Prés is the oldest in Paris. Watching the votive candles cast ghostly shadows on the walls, Robin and I wonder aloud about how dark it must have been in the church before the age of electricity. In a side chapel, a tombstone marks the burial place of René Descartes (1596-1650), the French philosopher and mathematician.

Outside now, we walk toward, and pause before, the "Magic Triangle"—Café de Flore, Les Deux Magots, and Brasserie Lipp, the watering holes of the literati—among whom numbered Ernest Hemingway, F. Scott Fitzgerald, Jean Paul Sartre, and Simone de Beauvoir.

We resume walking in the direction of Les Invalides, but decide we'd better stop to have some lunch. We've become much more mindful of the need

to plan around restaurant hours. For me—a *sandwiche mixte*. And here's a surprise . . . it's on a baguette.

After lunch we set out on the Boulevard des Invalides for the Hôtel which, we learn, was originally constructed under Louis XIV to house veterans. After the Hôtel and the original church, the Church of Saint-Louis, were completed, a third structure—the Dôme Church—was added to the complex. The Army Museum, housed in the north end of Les Invalides, contains an amazing array of armaments, recalling the zenith of French military might.

We enter the Dôme Church. After buying tickets, we take a few steps and immediately are at a balustrade looking down upon the layered tomb of Napoleon. In alcoves around his crypt, lit by somewhat garish orange and blue lights, are the tombs of his brothers Jerome and Joseph, his son Napoleon II, and many of the famous French generals. We walk down a staircase for another view of the reddish brown sarcophagus in which Napoleon's remains are encased.

. . . ghostly shadows . . .

The buildings that constitute the complex of the Hôtel des Invalides represent Paris's most imposing collection of monuments. Built in 1670 by Louis XIV, whose intention was to establish a hospital for disabled soldiers—*les invalides*, the structures mirror the grandeur of Versailles and bespeak the aspirations of empire. The most distinguishable of the buildings, the Dôme Church—whose gilded vault calls viewers throughout Paris to attention—harbors the remains of the country's best-known warrior, Napoleon I.

Before the existence of Les Invalides, many of those who had fought for the glory of France were forced, after fulfilling their duty, to join the ranks of the impoverished and rely on religious orders for housing. The new military hospital would remedy that situation with the construction of a compound, designed by Libéral Bruant, capable of accommodating 4000 residents. The architectural plan also called for erection of the Church of Saint-Louis of the Invalids, for use by the soldiers. Later the Sun King directed Hardouin-Mansart to design the Dôme church, one of the finest examples of the French classical style of architecture.

The Hôtel des Invalides is approached via an esplanade, which leads from the Quai d'Orsay, through a formal garden, to the entry. The complex houses the Museum of the Army, the Museum of Relief Maps and Plans, and the Museum of the Order of Liberation. In addition to Napoleon's ashes (reinterred at this site in 1861, after transport from the island of St. Helena) and the remains of other noted military figures, Les Invalides continues to house some surviving veterans from the two World Wars.

The Hôtel des Invalides

Image of Captain Dreyfus courtesy of the Bibliothèque Nationale de France.

Captain Alfred Dreyfus

In 1894 Captain Alfred Dreyfus, a French military officer, was arrested on charges of spying for Germany. Dreyfus, who was Jewish, was court martialed, convicted without having been allowed to view the evidence against him, publicly humiliated in a ritual during which he was stripped of his rank and medals, and sentenced to life imprisonment on Devil's Island.

The case erupted in a firestorm, with accusations of anti-Semitism being leveled at defenders of the Army's actions. Among the well-known supporters of Dreyfus were writers Émile Zola and Marcel Proust. Dreyfus was finally exonerated of the charges in 1906 and restored to his former military rank. He was later promoted to the rank of major and admitted to the order of the Legion of Honor.

Military Museum

This time we're looking up at it, a perspective that more convincingly conveys the power of this personage—the "Little Corporal," the self-crowned emperor.

We pass from the Dôme Church through a corridor to the Cour d'Honneur. Standing on this cobblestone courtyard, we're transported into the past. One hundred years ago, had we been standing here, we'd have witnessed the public humiliation of Captain Alfred Dreyfus.

In the Army Museum, we see the personal effects of Napoleon: his hat, coat, swords, battlefield encampment gear, and his white horse, Le Vizir, preserved for posterity by the skilled hands of a taxidermist. Most striking to me are other items that temporarily part the curtains of time—Napoleon's death mask, the room in which he died at Saint Helena, and a sweet looking little dog, also stuffed, that kept him company during his exile on Elba. Viewing these objects, I realize—in a way the grand sarcophagus could not make known to me—that, apart from the

. . . and a sweet looking little dog, also stuffed, that kept him company during his exile on Elba.

feats of the historical figure, there was a sentient person, Napoleon Bonaparte, who lived and breathed and occupied a certain space and time.

From Invalides, we head to the Musée Rodin, also known as the Hôtel Biron—recommended as a residence and studio to Rodin by the German poet, Rainer Maria Rilke. It's a large mansion with an entry garden in which, along with other works, is displayed *Le Penseur* (*The Thinker*). As we approach and walk around him, I notice that his hands look disproportionately large, which surprises me because Rodin is said to have concentrated special attention on the human hand.

In the house we see many of Rodin's famous sculptures: *Le Baiser* (*The Kiss*), and casts and models for *Les Bourgeois de Calais* (*The Burghers of Calais*) and *La Porte d'Enfer* (*The Gates of Hell*). As I look at the museum collection, I'm drawn to the works of Camille Claudel—the sister of poet Paul Claudel and a protégée, model, and mistress of Rodin—and I stare in

Auguste Rodin and Camille Claudel

Auguste Rodin (1840-1917), whose application to the École des Beaux Arts (School of Fine Arts) was rejected three times, went on to rank among the greatest of the French sculptors. He is believed to have helped resurrect what was then the dying art of sculpture, moving an academic emphasis on classical forms into the modern age. Rodin often sought to capture in his works a specific emotion, and his figures represent a dynamic of movement, interior tension, and psychological intensity.

The small body of work of Camille Claudel (1864-1943)—Rodin's muse, model, collaborator, and lover—is only in recent years being recognized for its own merit. Her artistic life is largely one of aspirations unrealized, as a consequence of opportunities denied to women at the turn of the century. Dependent on her relationship with Rodin to practice her art, Claudel experienced an emotional break and was committed to an asylum for the balance of her days after that relationship dissolved. Of his sister's talents, the poet Paul Claudel wrote: The art of Camille Claudel, from the first, glistens with the characteristics that are peculiarly her own: here we see the most powerful and the most naïve imagination taking its magnificent way—it is the gift of invention.

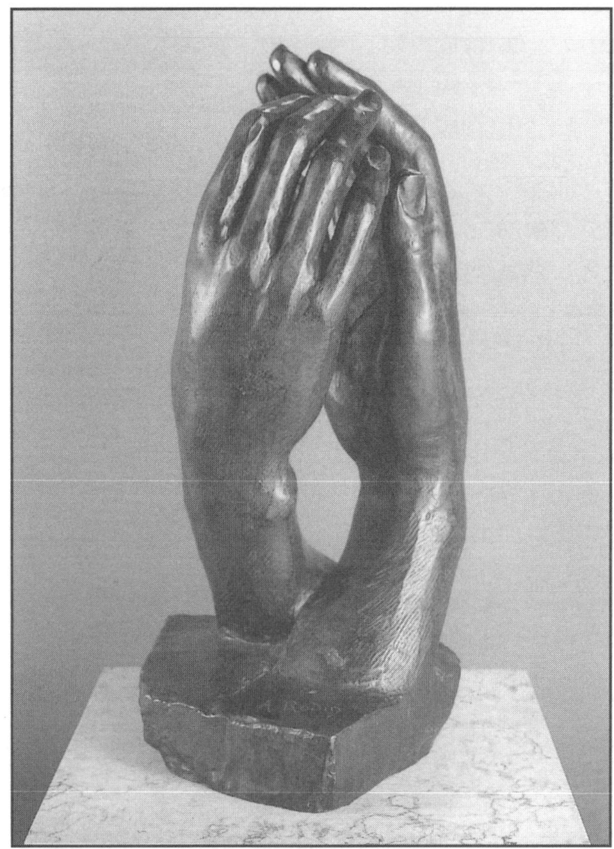

The Cathedral

Auguste Rodin: The Cathedral, 1910
Rodin Museum, Philadelphia; Gift of Jules E. Mastbaum.

Built for the Universal Exposition of 1889, the Eiffel Tower was—upon its completion— the tallest structure in the world, at 984 feet. And so it remained until 1930, when the Empire State Building surpassed it. Still, from the topmost of the tower's three viewing levels, one can see some 40 miles away.

The structure was designed by the engineer, Gustave Eiffel. It was selected as the winning entry in a competition that sought a monument to commemorate the centenary of the French Revolution. The tower's appearance on the Parisian landscape inspired strong sentiment: writers Émile Zola, Guy de Maupassant, and Alexandre Dumas (Fils) deplored it; Georges Seurat, Camille Pissarro, and Robert Delaunay felt compelled to paint it. Expected to be a temporary structure, the Eiffel Tower survived plans to demolish it by becoming a meteorologic and communications transmission station. Today, for people around the world, it has also become the symbol of Paris and all things French.

Across the Seine from the Eiffel Tower sits the Palais de Chaillot. This large structure, with its two curved wings, was built for the 1937 Paris Exhibition on the site which formerly held the Palais du Trocadero. The Trocadero, so named for the Spanish fort captured by the French in 1823, had served as an exhibition hall during the 1878 Exposition. The Palais de Chaillot houses a theater, a cinema, and four museums.

The Eiffel Tower and the Palais du Chaillot

disbelief at the small figures she was able to find in clay and jade. Sculpting has always been, for me, the most unfathomable of the arts. And Claudel really defies understanding with the detail she has captured. I'm wondering why there are so many sculptures of sad subjects in the museum—despair, misery. How do these emotions lend themselves to work in stone? Back out in the garden, we see the large *Bourgeois de Calais* and the *Porte d'Enfer*.

Now on to the Eiffel Tower. Robin and I see it peeking out from behind the buildings. We remember the stories we've heard about the controversies it sparked when it was built for the Exposition in 1889. It's not hard to imagine why it took the French a while to accept this structure. It's so huge an assertion of the modern age—its graceful iron filigree hovering over this city of classical forms.

We approach along the Champs de Mars, formerly a parade ground for cadets attending the nearby École Militaire. It's raining and windy. I'm afraid the wind will turn our umbrellas inside out. We're close enough now to see people at the three viewing levels. The third level looks extremely high. Neither Robin nor I am tempted to go up. We walk under and look through the middle of the tower, then on to the other side toward the Palais de Chaillot, with glances back to the tower.

Fountains in front of the Palais are beautiful, but Robin and I agree that the statuary and Neoclassical architectural style of the Palais project a cold, uninviting formality. Once again, we're surprised by the graffiti around this structure—originally built for the 1937 Exposition and now the location of several museums—and note that it seems a particularly popular spot with skaters and skateboarders. The view of the Eiffel Tower from here is great; the sun has come out.

We start down the Avenue Kleber, toward the Arc de Triomphe. Kleber is one of the twelve points of the Place de l'Étoile designed by Baron Haussman, and now referred to as the Place Charles de Gaulle.

> **The view of the Eiffel Tower from here is great; the sun has come out.**

graceful iron filigree...

The Arc de Triomphe— the Triumphal Arch—is the monumental anchor of the Place de l'Étoile, now known as the Place Charles de Gaulle. Commissioned by Napoleon I in 1806, the Arc de Triomphe is one of several edifices built by the emperor to memorialize his military campaigns and to honor his Grande Armée. The arch stands 164 feet high and measures 148 feet wide. Its pillars are decorated with giant friezes, the most well known of which is François Rude's *Departure of the Volunteers*, also called *The Marseillaise*. In 1920 the body of an Unknown Soldier was laid to rest in a tomb under the Arc de Triomphe in memory of the soldiers who died in World War I. An eternal flame of remembrance at the tomb, first lit in 1923, is rekindled each evening.

The square in which the Arc de Triomphe sits marks the convergence of 12 broad, radiating avenues, a design representative of the work of Baron Georges-Eugène Haussman, who served as the prefect of Paris and city planner under Napoleon III. Haussman effected bold changes in the layout of the city and is responsible, in large part, for its modern-day appearance.

The Arc de Triomphe in the Place Charles de Gaulle

The Arc is giant, ornate. We learn that, had Napoleon not changed his mind at the last minute, the monument might have been a giant elephant instead. We rest for a while near the Arc, trying to steel ourselves for crossing the street. Parisians drive like they're all practicing for the race at Le Mans; the merging of traffic at the Place Charles de Gaulle leaves us gasping, expecting disaster at any moment.

We survive crossing the street and start down the Champs Élysées. It's like Broadway, 5th Avenue, or Michigan Avenue—very much like the grandest street in a large American city. We decide to veer off the beaten path, heading north, off the Rond Point, along Franklin Roosevelt Avenue, for dinner at a little neighborhood spot, Le Ponthieu. Robin has a *croque monsieur*; I have ravioli, which neither conceals, nor is enclosed in, a baguette. Home on the metro, to the Hôtel de Ville stop, and a walk back to the Ile Saint-Louis. We fall into bed.

We rest for a while near the Arc, trying to steel ourselves for crossing the street.

Le Musée du Louvre and Le Musée d'Orsay

Again, we begin our day at the Sarah Bernhardt café with café au lait and croissants. Today's plans include the Musée du Louvre and the Musée d'Orsay. We'll try for a concert at the Sainte-Chapelle, if possible. Approaching from the Rue de Rivoli, we notice that there's a long line at the Louvre entrance, but it seems to be moving rapidly. Once in the Cour Napoleon, we marvel at the renovation project that's costing the French approximately $5 billion. They're cleaning the building's exterior, preparing more display areas and planning to offer more shopping and services. The Palais is incredible. It astounds me that people could ever have felt entitled to such opulence.

We move toward the I. M. Pei pyramid, a structure that, in my opinion, is completely out of keeping with the grandeur of the Louvre. It looks like an afterthought, something meant to be temporary until the real entrance is constructed. I notice, once

Construction of the Louvre began circa 1200 during the reign of Philippe-Auguste, who sought to build a feudal fortress capable of defending the city from invasion. Charles V, who reigned from 1364-1380, was responsible for expanding the fort and adapting it to serve as a royal residence. The palace was deserted, however, by the Valois kings during the Hundred Years War (1337-1453) with England. It was François I who, having agreed to live in the Louvre following his rescue from Italy, demolished the old keep and dungeon of the fortress and replaced those structures with a building in the Renaissance style. The Louvre was also expanded at the insistence of Catherine de Medici, as well as throughout the next three centuries under Henri II, Henri IV, Napoleon I, and Napoleon III.

The Louvre Museum

The palace became a museum in 1793, when the Revolutionary Convention decreed that the royal collections should be exhibited to the public. The Louvre currently houses approximately 400,000 works of art in seven different departments: Oriental Antiquities, Egyptian Antiquities, Greek and Roman Antiquities, Painting, Sculpture, Objets d'Art and Furniture, and Drawings. The I. M. Pei pyramid, the central entrance to the museum in the Cour Napoleon, was dedicated in 1989. Since 1989, the Louvre has undergone a reorganization of space designed to provide enlarged reception, service, and exhibition areas.

inside, that it also focuses the heat from the sunlight, like a prism, onto those of us waiting to buy tickets. But the line moves quickly, and we're soon in the museum.

We choose as our first destination the Sully section of the Louvre where we see the recently excavated foundations of the twelfth-century fortress of King Philippe-Auguste beneath the Cour Carrée. We enter the area of the dungeon, then the Salle Saint-Louis (the Saint Louis Room). How excited the workers on the excavation project must have been to uncover this lost treasure.

Heading upstairs, we encounter the 12-ton *Sphinx from Tanis*, then wander about to view the haunting *Tomb of Philippe Pot* and *Les Esclaves*— the *Dying Slave* and the *Rebellious Slave*—of Michaelangelo. We continue walking and soon are approaching the *Venus de Milo*. We observe her from multiple angles by virtue of a rotating pedestal. Truly, there is a grace and serenity in her attitude and expres-

sion. Next, we walk through the sculpture hall to see the *Torso of Man* in the Denon section. Robin and I wonder what distinguishes this work artistically from the many other torsos we see nearby.

We go up more stairs, turn, and there, dominating the stairway, is the *Victoire de Samothrace*. We sit on stairs nearby and read that she likely commemorates a naval victory. Her stance is assertive, triumphantly stepping into a wind that pushes her weighty wings behind her.

We leave to see the display of French crown jewels, but the room is closed. We pass *Samothrace* once more, and climb more stairs that lead through the rooms of the Dutch masters, through the Grand Galerie and past Watteau's *Gilles*, toward *La Joconde*. We come upon her suddenly, though we might have guessed she was near because of the crowd around. Tourists are snapping photos, despite multilingual requests that no pictures be taken. The portrait is smaller than its fame led me to expect. But the Mona

The *Venus de Milo*, the *Nike of Samothrace* (*Winged Victory*), and the *Mona Lisa* are among the most valued treasures of the Louvre's collection. Both the *Venus de Milo* and the *Samothrace* are Greek marble statues, dating from the Hellenistic period, i.e., from the third to the second centuries B.C. Specifically, the *Venus*—found in 1820 on the island of Milo in the Aegean Sea—is believed to have been created at the end of the second century. The statue is renowned as an example of female beauty.

The statue of Nike, the Greek goddess of victory, was found on the island of Samothraki in 1863 by Charles Champoiseau, the French consul at Adrianople. Champoiseau, also an archaeologist, happened upon the more than 100 fragments of the statue strewn about the island and sent them to the Louvre where they were assembled. The *Winged Victory* probably celebrates a Rhodian naval victory at the end of the third century.

Leonardo da Vinci's *Mona Lisa* is probably the world's most famous portrait. The painting is believed to represent Monna Lisa Gherardini who married the prominent Florentine, Francesco del Giocondo; thus, she is referred to in French as *La Joconde*. The work is thought to have been created around 1505 and was brought to Paris by da Vinci when he was summoned to the French court by François I.

The Venus de Milo

Lisa's smile *is* impenetrable; perhaps she's amused by the throng of humanity before her.

We see the works of the French Impressionists Monet, Manet, Pissarro. Also Renoir and Degas (ah, ballerinas). We decide to have a snack at the Café de Louvre before setting off for the Jardin de Tuileries and the Place de la Concorde. I'm gratified when the security guard tells me, in response to my request for directions to the café, that I speak French "*très bien.*"

On the way from the Louvre to the Jardin, we pass the Arc de Triomphe du Carrousel, built by Napoleon to commemorate, among other campaigns, his victory at Austerlitz. It's smaller than the Arc de Triomphe at the Place Charles de Gaulle. Walking toward the Tuileries Garden we can see, in the distance, the obelisk of the Place de la Concorde, framed by the backdrop of the Arc de Triomphe in the Étoile.

Entering the Tuileries Garden we look to the left and right at the beautiful symmetrical plantings of white tulips, supported by a bed of multicolored flow-ers. The plantings are arranged in the formal French style. There are fountains at both ends of the garden and, as we approach from the side nearest the Louvre, we see children sailing miniature boats on a pond, using sponge-tipped poles as prods.

It's windy now and the center aisle of the garden is not planted. The wind blows the sand and gravel into swirls. We walk on, parallel to the Seine, out of the garden, approaching the Place de la Concorde. That name confounds me, the place of peace . . . formerly, the Place de la Révolution. This is, of course, where the guillotine was set to work in the service of liberty, equality, and fraternity—with ripples that spread across Europe and into North America. I'm expecting something seismic. . .equivalent to the cataclysmic entry into the world of the social and political values embodied in the French Revolution. But today, there's only traffic; a clean, expansive square—the largest in Paris; tour buses; and a mute, apolitical, centuries-old Obelisk of Luxor effacing the history of this spot.

> . . . we see children sailing miniature boats on a pond, using sponge-tipped poles as prods.

. . . gravel into swirls

The Arc de Triomphe du Carrousel

The Arc de Triomphe du Carrousel and the Jardin des Tuileries

The Arc de Triomphe du Carrousel, with its marble, rose-colored columns, was built between 1806 and 1808 to commemorate the victories of Napoleon's army in Germany. Designed by Percier and Fontaine, the arch emulates a Roman prototype honoring the emperor Septimus Severus. The arch owes its name to its location, which was the site of royal pageants and parades—or *carrousels*—such as the one held in celebration of the birth of Louis XIV's first child.

The structure, which actually consists of three arches, measures 63 feet high and 75 feet wide. Originally, four bronze horses—taken by Napoleon from St. Mark's Cathedral in Venice—sat atop the arch. These were returned to Venice in 1815 following Napoleon's defeat, and replacements stand in their stead. The Arc de Triomphe du Carrousel forms part of La Voie Triomphal—the Triumphal Way—a grand axis of Paris along which is aligned, in addition to the Carrousel Arch, the Obelisk of Luxor at the Place de la Concorde, the Champs Élysées, the Arc de Triomphe at the Étoile, and the modern Grande Arche de la Défense.

Between the Arc de Triomphe du Carrousel and the Place de la Concorde lies the Jardin des Tuileries—the Tuileries Garden. Built on the site of a tile works (*tuileries*), the sixty-acre garden was begun by Pierre Le Nôtre at the request of Maria de Medici who wanted a formal park similar to the Florentine gardens with which she was familiar. The Tuileries was later redesigned by André Le Nôtre, gardener for Louis XIV. Originally, the garden lay before the queen's residence—the former Palais des Tuileries, which was set afire in 1871 by the Communards and later demolished during the Third Republic. The western end of the garden is flanked by two pavilions: the Orangerie—a former citrus nursery turned museum—and the Jeu du Palme, the one-time royal tennis courts now used as an exhibition space.

Covering more than 20 acres between the Champs Élysées and the Tuileries, the Place de la Concorde is the largest square in Paris. Designed by the architect Gabriel, the square was originally known as the Place Louis XV, as it had been chosen as the site for an equestrian statue of the king. The more well-known use of the square—as the stage upon which some of the infamous acts of the Revolution were performed—was presaged, perhaps, in the trampling deaths of more than 100 spectators at a fireworks display on the occasion of the marriage of Louis XVI to Marie Antoinette. In 1793, the square became the Place de la Révolution, wherein some 1300 persons—including the king and queen and, eventually, the leaders of the Reign of Terror, Danton and Robespierre—were beheaded.

In 1795, the Directory renamed the square the Place de la Concorde. Today, in the center of the square stands the 3300-year-old Obelisk of Luxor, presented in 1829 to Charles X (and erected in 1833 during the reign of Louis Philippe) by the Egyptian viceroy, Mehmed Ali. Also within the square are two fountains modeled after those in St. Peter's Square in Rome. At the four corners of the Place de la Concorde are statues representing the eight major cities of France.

The Place de la Concorde

We cross the Seine and start toward the Musée d'Orsay. We pass the building where the French National Assembly sits, then the Museum of the Legion of Honor, and the Musée d'Orsay is before us. Formerly it was the Gare d'Orsay, now transformed into a magnificent jewel case of visual art. The works are beautifully displayed and we are struck by the impression that this museum rivals the Louvre in the wealth of its collection. It deserves far more time than we've allotted today. We see more paintings of the Impressionists and an underground, scale model of the Opéra.

We decide to stop for a cup of coffee at the Café des Hauteurs on the upper level. Mindful of the time, Robin asks me how late it's getting, before realizing that—just behind us—is probably the largest clock either of us has ever seen.

We return to the exhibits to view the painting of *Whistler's Mother* and a display of art deco furniture. We know that the museum will be closing soon, but just as we are about to leave, we notice in a brochure, the picture of Marcel Proust by Jacques-Émile Blanche. We scurry about, unsuccessfully, to find it, while hoping that we'll have the chance to return to the museum during this visit.

We walk in the direction of the Sainte-Chapelle to inquire about a 5:45 P.M. organ concert (it's already 6:00). The gendarme tells us that the Sainte-Chapelle, along with the entire Palais de Justice complex, is closed. We decide to return to the hotel, rest for a bit, and make plans for dinner. We opt for someplace nearby and plan to ask at the desk for a reservation.

At the desk is Patricia, with whom we strike up a conversation. She is from Italy, she tells us. She's been in France for five years. We're surprised because her French has no trace of an accent and she seems very French in her manner. As we ask about the historic richness of her own country, she tells us that she is from the north of Italy and describes the south as crime-ridden and dangerous. While we're talking, a man from the Montecristo Restaurant, down the

Formerly a rail-way station, the old Gare d'Orsay is now a bridge—temporally—between the Louvre and the Pompidou. Built on the site of what was the Palais d'Orsay—one of the structures destroyed by fire during the civil conflict of 1871, the station and railway hotel were constructed as a terminus for the Orléans line. After fewer than forty years' operation, however, the Gare d'Orsay was abandoned because of the need for longer rail platforms. The structure was saved from demolition in 1971 with its designation as an historic landmark.

The movement to convert the Gare d'Orsay to a museum was begun under President Georges Pompidou and realized by his successor, Valéry Giscard d'Estaing. Works dating from 1848 to 1914 were transferred to the renovated structure from the Louvre, the Palais de Tokyo, the Jeu du Palme, and the Orangerie creating—upon its opening in 1986—the Musée d'Orsay with its spectacular collection of nineteenth-century art. Among the art forms represented in the collection are painting, sculpture, architecture, furniture, graphic arts, photography, and decorative arts. Presentation of the art within the museum is enhanced not only by the beauty of the setting but also by the provision of each work's cultural context.

The Musée d'Orsay

block, comes in to say hello to Patricia. After he leaves, we ask her for a recommendation for dinner. She says the Montecristo is terrific and offers to call the person who just left, her friend Kamel, who'll give us a good table.

We decide to go to the Montecristo in about a half hour, after we walk to the public phone and call Artie and Michael. We find a pay phone near the Hôtel de Ville, pop in our *télécartes* and talk quickly, so as not to expend all of our phone card units. After hanging up, we spend a few moments looking at the Hôtel de Ville—the town hall and the official residence of the mayor of Paris. Though far more elaborate than the Saint Louis City Hall, the Hôtel de Ville reminds us of the Saint Louis structure, which was modeled after its Parisian counterpart.

Dinner at the Montecristo is memorable. Kamel greets us at the door and leads us to a table. The restaurant is small, charming. I decide to have the same dish that a man nearby is having—a lemon

> **. . . the same dish that a man nearby is having— a lemon pasta . . . mmmm, delicious.**

pasta . . . mmmm, delicious. The entrée is Veal Milanese, followed by a luscious cherry ice cream dessert. At dinner, we meet two Americans from Houston, Terry and Patti. They recount a horror story about their flight over. I'm reminded that our own return trip looms in the near future. After dinner, it's back to the hotel where I scribble a few journal notes and we take account of our funds to prepare for the next day.

April 27

On the Ile de la Cité

This morning we decide to try a café on the corner of the Rue Saint-Louis en l'Ile for breakfast. Our waiter is pleasant and playful, although I see his expression and demeanor change in response to a running-suit clad American couple who ask brusquely, in English, for "a ham sandwich and a glass of orange juice." No "please," no "thank you." I ask for another

The Hôtel de Ville

Trade Guild House at which the powerful association of water merchants met to discuss and regulate the movement of goods along the Seine. In 1357, Étienne Marcel—a wealthy clothier and the provost of merchants—bought the House of Pillars, which sat on the present site of the Hôtel de Ville. From this location, Marcel, a member of the Estates General—a group of royalty, clergy, and merchants convoked by the King in times of financial distress—undertook an unsuccessful attempt to launch governmental reforms in defiance of the monarchy.

The Place de Grève—now the Place de l'Hôtel de Ville— lay before the House of Pillars and, in addition to becoming a port for the unloading of wares, was also the setting of a market, of laborers' grievances, of public feasts, and public executions.

Construction of the first city hall began in 1553 under François I and was completed during the reign of Louis XIII. During the Revolution, the building was occupied by the ruling assembly. In 1835 two wings were added to the town hall, but 36 years later the Communards set fire to the structure. The Hôtel de Ville was rebuilt during the Third Republic following the fall of the Communards under the direction of the architects Ballu and Deperthes. Today the city hall serves not only as the seat of municipal power, but also as the residence of the mayor of Paris, and as the city's official reception hall.

The site on which the current Hôtel de Ville rests has been home to the town hall of Paris for more than three centuries. But even before the establishment of an official city hall, the area was the scene of events reflecting the exercise of power by the populace.

The forerunner to the city hall—and its town council—was the Merchants

cup of coffee and he teases me saying, "*c'est impossible*," it's absolutely impossible—one cup to a customer. Drinking my refill, I realize I'm addicted to café au lait.

After breakfast we're off to the bank to exchange travelers' checks for francs. The little Société Générale on the Ile Saint-Louis isn't able to do the exchange, so—with the assistance and brief escort of a bank customer—we head for another of its branches on the Ile de la Cité. Because it's almost lunchtime, during which the bank may be closed, we walk toward Notre Dame Cathedral.

Outside, near the front of the cathedral, there's a little display showing construction of the church, undertaken in the twelfth century. Guild workers are depicted cutting and carving the stone, then using winches to hoist it into place. Looking at those primitive methods, it's almost impossible to imagine that they could be used to produce the structure that we see before us.

Robin and I enter the cathedral and, after our eyes adjust to the lack of light, we look down the long nave toward the high altar, marveling at the vaulted ceiling. Walking down a side aisle, we stop at the transept to study the north and south rose windows and see, in the south transept, the most well-known statue in Notre Dame—that of the Virgin and Child. We move nearer the altar to observe at close range the sculpted friezes behind the choir. Finally, we enter the cathedral museum to view the relics housed there, which are said to include pieces of the True Cross and of the Crown of Thorns. As we leave Notre Dame, we recall that every important moment of French history was celebrated in and around this church. And I'm quietly grateful that, through the lens of my own Roman Catholic upbringing, I can see not only the historical significance of the cathedral, but I can also sense the reverence that inspired, and is reflected within, it.

Drinking my refill, I realize I'm addicted to café au lait.

"c'est impossible,"

The Cathedral of Notre Dame in Paris—probably the most recognizable church in the world—is the gravitational center of French religious life. And as religion has been so inextricably a part of French history, the stones of this great cathedral bear silent witness to the nation's most important events.

Construction of Notre Dame began in 1163 on a site that had long been hallowed ground. A temple to Jupiter stood on this spot when Gaul was under Roman control. That structure is believed to have been succeeded by two churches before Notre Dame was built: one dedicated to Saint-Étienne (constructed in the fifth or sixth century) and a second dedicated to Mary (erected in the seventh century).

Notre Dame Cathedral, based on design sketches prepared by Maurice de Sully—the bishop of Paris, is predominantly Gothic in architectural style, though it contains some Romanesque elements. Among its most well-known features are the flying buttresses, the gargoyles, and the breathtaking rose windows. Its foundation stone is said to have been laid by Pope Alexandre III. Construction of the cathedral, which was begun by the master builders Pierre de Monterreau and Jean de Chelles, required two centuries to complete.

It was from Notre Dame that the crusaders set off for the holy wars. In 1302, King Philip the Fair convened the first Estates General in the cathedral. Henry VI of England was crowned in Notre Dame in 1430. By the end of the seventeenth century, the cathedral began to be subject to destructive changes, including the removal of some of its stained glass, and during the Revolution—when it was transformed to a temple of reason—it suffered significant damage. Finally, after serving as the site of Napoleon's self-coronation, Notre Dame became the beneficiary of renovation under the direction of Viollet le Duc, who contributed the spire, the sacristy, replicas of the Kings of Judah, and the statues that overlook the city from the roof.

In the twentieth century, Notre Dame was the place

The Western Rose Window at Notre Dame Cathedral

from which General Charles de Gaulle called upon the nation, in 1944, to give thanks for its liberation from wartime occupation. De Gaulle would return to the cathedral a last time, in 1970, on the occasion of the celebration of his requiem mass. Today Notre Dame Cathedral—this vessel for millions of votives—offers a reassuring constancy, as the years stream past.

From Notre Dame we take another try—successfully, this time—at exchanging dollars for francs, then we're off in the direction of the Conciergerie. Because we're not expecting to find a restaurant in the Conciergerie *(and who would want to eat in it if there were one)*, we stroll over to the Place Dauphine to a little restaurant hidden from the main thoroughfare of the Pont Neuf—the Bar du Caveau. It's small, delightful, with good food.

The Conciergerie was built as a royal residence, then later was used to detain prisoners. It saw much of its activity during the Revolution when it housed Marie Antoinette, Charlotte Corday and, eventually, Robespierre and Danton, among others. We see the huge Salle des Gens d'Armes and the kitchen capable of serving 3000 royal guests. We view a room similar to the one in which Marie Antoinette was kept. We visit the Cour des Femmes (the women's exercise yard) and the Chapelle d'Expiation, where the Girondins (members of the French legislative assem-

bly in 1791 who sought democratic reform) spent their last night. The Conciergerie is scary to visit; it's dark, dank, there are bars at the windows and it's not hard to imagine the terror of those who were brought here to await a meeting with Monsieur de Paris (the executioner).

From the Conciergerie, we start toward the Musée de Cluny, through the Latin Quarter, where students crowd the streets. We get to the museum one half hour before closing, but they allow us to enter. We look around quickly at the *Lady with the Unicorn* tapestries, see the sculpted heads of the Kings of Judah (from Notre Dame Cathedral), and wish for more time.

Now hurrying past the Sorbonne and the Université de Paris, we walk toward the Panthéon. We're surprised at how contained and inaccessible the university area is.

The Panthéon is closed. We look at the inscription on the front of the building "to the great

...bars at the windows...

The Conciergerie, with its somber exterior facing the Seine, forms part of the complex of the Palais de Justice on the Ile de la Cité. The Conciergerie was built by Philippe le Bel, circa 1300, as a royal residence. It was the seat of power for the kings of France until Charles V moved the court to the Marais, leaving the concierge—the king's constable—in charge of the palace. In 1391, the Conciergerie became a palace prison and then, in the 16th century, a state prison. Initially, it was used to confine prisoners who had the distinction of committing the most notorious crimes. For example, François Ravaillac, the assassin of Henri IV, was incarcerated there in 1610. But during the French Revolution, the population of the Conciergerie swelled to include thousands of detainees who were held there while awaiting death by the guillotine.

The structure ceased being a prison in 1914, though the forbidding facade of the Conciergerie is a ready reminder of its history. Today, the great Gothic halls of the former palace and prison—often the scene of musical and theatrical performances—reverberate with far happier sounds.

The Conciergerie

men, a grateful country" and walk around the exterior thinking about the remains of those inside—Voltaire, Rousseau, Zola, Hugo. I feel heartened that France holds its great writers and thinkers in such high esteem. Across the street from the Panthéon is Saint-Étienne du Mont, a church that we later learn has the tombs of Pascal, Racine, and Marat.

We turn back toward the Jardin du Luxembourg and have a seat before the fountain and the pond to rest for a bit. The Palais is to the right . . . another French monument undergoing renovation and temporarily off limits.

Time for dinner. We choose a place at the intersection of the "Boul Mich" and Boulevard Saint-Germain called Café de Cluny. We'll get back to the hotel a bit early this evening. Our first early night in.

April 28

More Places and a Little Drama

We're having trouble waking at a normal

hour. It's hard to get out of bed before 8:30 or 9:00 A.M., probably because we haven't entirely adjusted to the schedule. And (*come to think of it*) we're doing a tremendous lot of walking each day. We start the day with breakfast at our neighborhood café, noticing en route how cold it is this morning.

We decide we'd better get to the Gare Montparnasse to get information about Illiers/Combray. The information clerk asks me "*Qu'est-ce que là-bas?*" I tell her there's a Proust museum. We'll have to go through Chartres, so we plan to visit the cathedral while there. We go to the *guichet* (booking office) to purchase tickets and I ask the clerk about the special fare we've heard is available if two people are traveling together. He says it's really reserved for members of the same family. I tell him Robin and I aren't in the same family. He and I start laughing; he's blushing. We get our tickets and are set for the next day.

The Panthéon was conceived as a vow. King Louis XV promised that, should he recover from an episode of illness, he would build a church to honor Sainte-Geneviève—the patron saint of Paris who is credited with having defended the city, by encouraging its inhabitants to pray, from invasion by Attila the Hun. Restored to health, Louis XV directed the architect Soufflot to oversee construction of the church, the classical design of which imitated the Pantheon in Rome.

The Panthéon

Completion of the project, in 1789, coincided with the start of the Revolution; thus, the church was converted to a secular use—a mausoleum for the "great men who died in the period of the liberty of France." The building alternated between being a church and a mausoleum until the end of the nineteenth century, when its role as a nonreligious burial place prevailed. The crypt contains the remains of Voltaire, Rousseau, Hugo, and Zola. With its windows covered and a weighty 272-foot dome piercing the sky, the Panthéon dominates the eastern Left Bank, casting its stoic shadow on the streets below.

Now we're off, past the Jardin des Plantes, across the Seine to the Place de la Bastille. All that marks the spot of the prison is the towering July Column. The prison itself was dismantled as the hated symbol of oppression during the Revolution. Near the July Column, the sun turns the panes of the new, modern Paris Opéra de la Bastille to gold.

We walk along the Rue de Bastille toward a side street that will lead us to the Place des Vosges, called the prettiest square in Paris. It's also the oldest and part of what had been the aristocratic section of Paris—the Marais. We see the former residences of Victor Hugo and Théophile Gautier.

It's lunchtime, so we stop into a little restaurant on the Place des Vosges called Eurydice. We order steaming, big bowls of chili, along with tea and bread, and listen to Billie Holiday sing Gershwin. It's still rather cold out, so the chili hits the spot. In a little shop around the corner from the restaurant, Robin buys a scarf and I look for a hat.

We order steaming, big bowls of chili, along with tea and bread, and listen to Billie Holiday sing Gershwin.

After lunch we decide, since we're in the neighborhood, to visit the Musée Carnavalet. This museum's collection presents the history of the City of Paris. Madame de Sévigné lived for 20 years in the building that houses the museum. We walk through and see rooms reconstructed from the period of Louis XVI, also articles from the Revolution, including locks of hair from the King (Louis XVI) and Marie Antoinette. We're hurrying through to try to get to Père Lachaise before it closes. On the way out of the museum, we pop into the gift store to look for souvenirs and Robin notices a book about the museum that shows an exhibit entitled *Les Chambres des Écrivains*—the writers' rooms. There, in a photograph, is a reconstruction of Proust's room. We race back into the museum, upstairs through the Grand Galerie, past the bed chamber of Anna de Noailles and there it is. A reconstruction of the cork-lined room, with Proust's personal effects—his bed, covered with a blue satin spread; lamp; nightstand, on which are placed

We race back...

The Bastille St. Antoine, whose destruction—as symbolic of French independence—is commemorated annually, was built on order of Charles V as part of a fortress designed to defend the eastern edge of fourteenth-century Paris. During the reign of Louis XIII, Cardinal Richelieu—the king's minister—demolished most of the fortress except for the Bastille, which was reserved for use as a state prison. There political prisoners could be held without trial; consequently, the Bastille came to represent

The July Column in the Place de la Bastille

the arbitrary exercise of the power of the monarchy. On July 14, 1789, after pillaging the arsenal at Invalides, a mob stormed the Bastille, triggering a series of events that would topple Louis XVI. During the attack on the prison, its last seven occupants were set free and the prison commander—de Launay—was killed. Shortly thereafter the prison itself was razed.

In memory of those who died in the Revolutions of 1830 and 1848, the July Column—atop which stands the Spirit of Liberty—was erected. In 1989, in celebration of the Bicentennial of the French Revolution, the new Bastille Opera—the opera house for the people—opened at the location where the old prison once stood. The Place de la Bastille continues to be a site of demonstration for political protestors.

The Place des Vosges——behind whose inexpressive facades the bygone merriment of lords and ladies faintly echoes—lies within the eastern part of the Marais district. Originally called the Place Royale, the square consists of thirty-six stately mansions, capped with Mansard roofs, constructed over a series of arcades, and surrounding a formal garden. Design of the square—a visual delight to the geometricians among us—was undertaken in 1605 during the reign of Henri IV; it was completed in 1612 in conjunction with the marriage of Henri's son, Louis XIII, to Anne of Austria. In addition to the *pavillons* of the king and queen, the residences of other notables lining the Place des Vosges included those of the novelist, Alphonse Daudet; the dramatists, Pierre Corneille and Jean Baptiste Moliere; and the cardinal and statesman, the Duc de Richelieu. Today, the arcades shelter a variety of boutiques, antique shops, and restaurants.

The Place des Vosges

One of the most interesting attractions in Paris, the Museum of History of the City of Paris (the Musée Carnavalet) occupies two neighboring mansions in the Marais district—the Hôtel Carnavalet and the Hôtel le Peletier de Saint-Fargeau. Objects within the museum provide an experience of immersion into the day-to-day lives of Parisians from Roman times to the Belle Époque.

Madame la Marquise de Sévigné

Image of Madame de Sévigné from the Post Office of France, issue #642i, design #2198

These pieces include not just paintings and sculptures but street signs and shop signs, rooms furnished with period furniture, business and household articles.

The main portion of the museum, the Hôtel Carnavalet, was built in 1548. From 1677 to 1696, the Hôtel Carnavalet served as the residence of Madame la Marquise de Sévigné, who played hostess to many of the great minds of her time. For 25 years, Madame la Marquise chronicled French popular culture in more than 1500 letters to her daughter, whose marriage had taken her to Provence. In 1880, the Hôtel Carnavalet was converted to its current use. The museum was enlarged in 1989 with the annexation of the adjacent mansion.

his *cahiers* (notebooks); dressing table; cane; and chaise longue. We're bowled over.

We'll barely make Père Lachaise today and finally decide to postpone our visit there until Thursday, when we have more time. We'll take the metro to Montmartre to see Sacré Coeur instead.

Ready to get the metro, we're detained by a bit of drama. Robin notices a woman getting on a train and sees the train door close before the woman's child, a little girl of about nine, can get inside. We talk with the little girl, who appears frightened but relatively calm, and try to learn her name and where she lives. We need to decide whether to put her on the train for the next station or to wait with her there. A third woman is nearby and talks with the girl. We conclude it will be better to wait with her there for her mother to return. The girl lives in Saint-Denis, so we consider the possibility of having to take her home if her mother doesn't arrive. About ten minutes pass. Finally, *sa mère arrive*. She and the little girl look

Ready to get the metro, we're detained by a bit of drama.

happy and relieved. We continue on our way to Sacré Coeur.

The basilica is a fairly spectacular sight—a tiered wedding cake—on top of the hill. The view of Paris is exquisite from here. We go inside to rest and are amazed by the three huge domes. With May approaching, flowers adorn and surround the statue of Mary.

Outside now, we notice that, instead of walking, we can "funiculate" down the hill. We choose the stairs while kids next to us race down a steep incline. Dinner is in a small Montmartre café.

April 29

Chartres and Illiers/Combray

We have breakfast at the hotel so that we can get to the Gare Montparnasse to catch the train to Illiers/Combray. We have just a bit more than an hour in Chartres on the way to Illiers and plan to stop to see the cathedral. The ride is interesting; we see many

…three huge domes.

Just as one can see the whole of Paris from the steps of the Basilica of the Sacred Heart, so, too, the towering white domes of this landmark are visible throughout the city. The church was built—following the French defeat in the Franco-Prussian War and ensuing civil upheaval—as an act of hope and of atonement for a lack of spirituality, which some regarded as the real cause of the nation's problems.

Construction of the Roman-Byzantine style basilica, which sits atop the Butte Montmartre, was begun in 1875—according to the plan of the architect, Paul Abadie— and financed by every parish in France. The huge mosaic of the vault was created between 1900 and 1922, although the basilica was officially consecrated in 1919, at the conclusion of the first World War. In the bell tower hangs one of the largest bells ever cast— the 19-ton "Savoyarde." The Basilica of the Sacred Heart, since 1885, has been a site of perpetual prayer and a place of pilgrimage.

The Basilica of the Sacred Heart

very old communities, each, we guess, with its own history. We're also surprised about the graffiti that extends far beyond the *banlieu* (suburbs) of the city of Paris.

It feels good to settle in on the train, after a few hair-raising minutes while boarding. We were scheduled to leave at 9:29 A.M., but the gate from which the train was leaving wasn't announced until 9:26. We had a mad scramble. But there's time now for reading the *International Herald Tribune* and finishing some post cards. I'm eager to see (and am anxious about) the accounts, in the newspaper, of rioting in Los Angeles in response to the Rodney King case. The French, when they learn we're Americans, express their concern about these troubling events.

The cathedral's spire is visible in the distance. We arrive in Chartres at 11:30 A.M. and walk up the hill from the SNCF station (the national railway), after a café and bathroom break, to the cathedral. I didn't realize that the complete name is the Cathédrale de Notre Dame de Chartres. It is, perhaps, more breathtaking than Notre Dame de Paris and more representative of the Gothic style. We sit in the church for a while, I buy a souvenir, then we walk back to the station.

Fortunately, as we get off the train in Illiers, a woman and her child, who live in the town, offer to direct us to the Centre Ville (downtown), where the house of Proust's family is located. She says there are many visitors to Illiers. She guesses that about 2000 people live here.

There's little traffic. We walk along a bit farther with the woman until she shows us a left turn that will lead us to the Proust family residence, referred to in his massive *chef d'oeuvre* as the home of Tante Léonie. She says that the church, called Saint-Hilaire by Proust, but actually named Saint-Jacques, is nearby.

A striking feature of this town—there are no other people around. We continue to walk until, sud-

The cathedral's spire is visible in the distance.

...a mad scramble.

So convincing is the illusion of Gothic lightness that the Cathedral of Chartres seems to hover above the fields of wheat that surround it. The west front of the church reflects what had once been a Romanesque-style structure, begun in 1020. After its destruction in 1194 by fire, the present Gothic cathedral was superimposed on the remains of the original church. With the exception of the second bell tower, added in the sixteenth century, Chartres has undergone few changes. Among its other features, the cathedral is famous for its collection of twelfth- and thirteenth-century stained glass windows.

Figures from the Facade of the Chartres Cathedral

The Church of St. Jacques in Illiers/Combray

The writer, Marcel Proust— regarded as one of the most important literary figures of the twentieth century—spent holidays at his uncle's home in Illiers. In his massive work, *Remembrance of Things Past*, Proust transforms Illiers into the fictional town of Combray and renames St. Jacques—whose asymmetrical towers can be seen when approaching Illiers—St. Hilaire.

denly, we notice in one of the narrow streets, a sign above a fairly unimposing building, La Maison de Tante Léonie. We cross to the house and see a sign next to the door that says that tours begin at 3:00, 4:00, and 5:00 P.M. It's now 1:00 P.M. and the house, shutters and all, is locked up tight. Across from Tante Léonie's is the Syndicat d'Initiative—the tourist's bureau. Its sign reads, "*Fermée.*" Little did we know we had arrived during lunch, when everything closes between 12:00 and 2:00 P.M.

We decide to look for the church. It's just around the corner, with asymmetrical towers looming. It's in the center of the square that Proust describes in recounting his outings with his family.

We go around the block and up the street a bit. The door to the neighborhood *pâtisserie* is open. We go in and ring for assistance. The baker tells us that this is the bakery from which Tante Léonie bought her madeleines, confirming a sign outside. We're not sure about this claim, but we get some and

The madeleines have a lemon flavor . . .

sample them as we return to Tante Léonie's house. The madeleines have a lemon flavor and are soft, like cake.

The house has not yet opened. It's so disappointing to imagine that we've come eighty kilometers to see this and now can't get in. We've planned to take the 1:30 P.M. train. Luckily, it dawns on us that we needn't be so schedule-bound and can, in fact, just remain at Illiers until the last train leaves at 6:00 P.M. We decide to have lunch at a nearby café and return.

When we get back at about five minutes to three, a man is waiting to go in. A good sign, the shutters are open now. Three o'clock comes and goes. . .five minutes after three. . . ten after. . .we're still waiting. Finally, the man decides to ring the bell. A woman answers the door and says with a rather stern voice that we are too late, the tour has already begun. Others arrive after us and get the same reply. We'll try once more and plan to return at 3:45 P.M. We find another little café/tabac, have some coffee and talk with a local woman, the proprietress, about Proust

A good sign . . .

The garden of Jules Amiot—called the Pré Catalan—is adjacent to the family home in Illiers. It is believed to have provided the inspiration for a similar setting described in Proust's masterpiece—the garden of the character, Charles Swann. The path to Swann's, Swann's Way, was one of two routes chosen—according to the protagonist and narrator, Marcel—for family walks and is symbolic of the fulfillment of the artistic life. The other route—the Guermantes Way—represents upward mobility, social aspirations, and acceptance by the aristocracy.

The Garden of Proust's Uncle, Jules Amiot

and visitors to the museum. She gives us some printed information to keep.

We're positioned on the steps across from the house, determined, this time, to get in. At 3:50, the doors open and two women greet us pleasantly. We mention that a man had been waiting with us, before 3:00, and that perhaps he'll return. They collect our admission and we walk to a glass-enclosed area, like a solarium, in back of the house. The guide is fluent in French and English. Three other people join us, all of whom speak English, so she conducts the tour in English, occasionally interjecting some French phrases. She asks if we're familiar with the writer, if we've read any of his work. Robin and I, having just completed Proust in our reading group, have been waiting for someone—anyone—to ask this question. "Yes," we answer in unison, "all of *À La Recherche du Temps Perdu*." She's obviously impressed. We love it.

The solarium is surrounded with photos of Proust, his family, and friends. The guide tells us how Madame de Chevigné and the Baron Montesquieu, when they recognized themselves in Proust's novel, were hurt and never really forgave him for it.

Now she leads us through the house, the sitting room, the dining room and up the stairs (which we remember from Proust's account in the novel of the night Swann's visit prevented Marcel from receiving his mother's goodnight kiss). The guide leads us to the room in which Proust slept during his visits there. She reminds us that these visits occurred when he was between the ages of six and nine. In his room we see a bed with a canopy, a dressing table, a prie-dieu, a fireplace with a clock on the mantle, and the magic lantern (a kerosene lamp with a protrusion for inserting slides that are then projected on the wall). She tells us that the room used to be bigger before indoor plumbing was installed. During Proust's childhood visits, the W.C. was in back of the house.

Next, we're led to Tante Léonie's room. There's a single bed near the window and, next to it, a

She's obviously impressed. We love it.

...the magic lantern...

sealed glass case with Tante Léonie's prayer book, a madeleine, her tea cup and *tilleul* (lime blossom tea). We learn that Tante Léonie (in real life, Proust's Aunt Elisabeth) was not a widow, had three children, and was not hypochondriacal. The guide says that Tante Léonie's character was probably based more on the paternal grandmother.

Up to the third floor now, to a room that houses more photos and an illustration of Proust's family tree. The guide contrasts the writer's maternal grandparents, wealthy Parisians, with the paternal grandparents, bourgeoisie who owned a nearby store. We watch a brief video about Proust and the tour is over. We pick out a few souvenirs in the gift shop and head toward the train station.

Across from the station we stop at a café, Les Guermantes, for something to drink. Inside we meet the owner and two residents of Illiers, one of whom helps out at the café. They're walking billboards for Illiers and warn us that Paris is "*pas bon.*" They also

> ... "très, très, très, très, jolie ... très sublime."

clue us into other attractions at Chartres, including La Maison de Picassiette, a complex constructed entirely from colorful shards of broken glass. The helper describes this attraction as "*très, très, très, très jolie . . . très sublime.*" Their criticisms of city living are fun. We finish our drinks; they ask us to promise to return. We say we will, when the hawthorns are in bloom, and we cross to the station.

We're about ten minutes early for the train. I ask the information clerk if we need to validate our tickets again. We're waiting outside the terminal when he calls out, "*à Paris.*" We hop on the train, but wonder why, given the terribly punctual French railway system, the train for Paris has arrived before the train for Bordeaux. We also wonder if the train will soon turn around, because it seems to be headed in the wrong direction. After a few more minutes, we decide to check with another passenger and learn that the train we're on is going to Bordeaux. We jump off, run over to the next track, and ask if that train is going to

. . . wrong direction.

Paris. It is. We board with less than thirty seconds before the train takes off down the track.

Back in Paris, we get the metro to Châtelet. Walking toward the Ile Saint-Louis, we stop in a small dark café along the Seine. Something that sounds like Moroccan music is playing and hanging on the walls are various Mexican and Middle Eastern objects. We brand it "generic ethnic," order big bowls of pasta and, of course, wine. It's been another long and eventful day.

April 30
Shopping, Père Lachaise, and Vivaldi

Today we're pooped and poking around. After breakfast we change more travelers' checks for francs, for a possible trip to Saint-Étienne, though Robin hasn't yet been able to reach her friends Marie and Brigitte. The banks will be closed tomorrow for *Le Ier mai* (the May 1st holiday) and will close today at noon.

…in the rooftop café overlooking the Seine.

Now we're off to La Samaritaine, *un grand magasin* (department store), to look for souvenirs and a few personal items. Along the way we visit several *papeteries* (stationers) and a violin shop so that I can buy some rosin for Artie.

The Samaritaine is like a U.S. department store, just more tightly packed. I buy some patterned French tights and Robin finds some dishtowels for her grandmother. We have a delicious lunch of *poulet rôti et pommes frites* (roast chicken and fried potatoes) in the rooftop café, overlooking the Seine.

It's after 3:00 P.M. now and we'll have to beat a path over to Père Lachaise before it closes. It's a long walk to the Place de la Bastille, from which we head uphill to the cemetery. We start toward Proust's grave in section 85. On the way, we encounter a young man who's looking for the tomb of Jim Morrison. Suddenly, there with directions is a small elderly man who, we later decide, is Vincent de Langlade; he's written a dozen books about Père

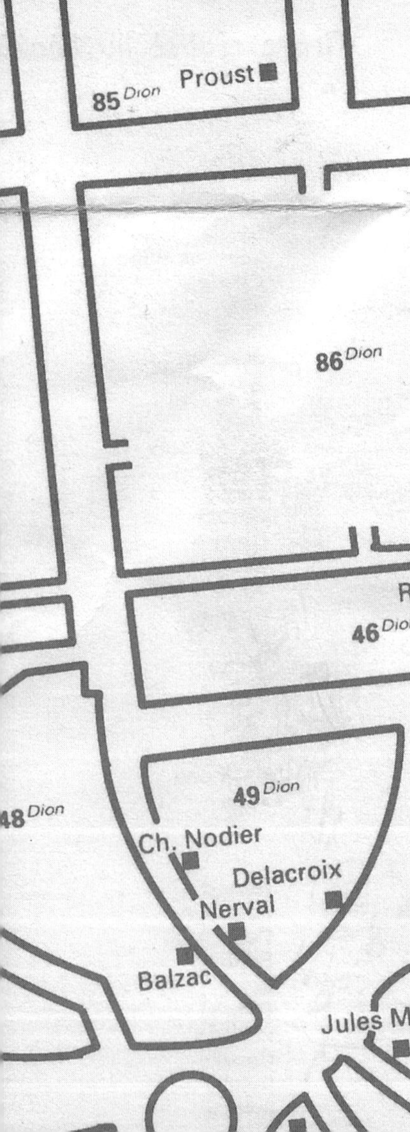

Père Lachaise Cemetery

Who can quite understand the popularity of a cemetery as an attraction for the living? But Père Lachaise with its 100,000 sepulchres is said to receive a million visitors a year. Of course, there's the allure of the tranquil setting, the incredible burial monuments and statuary, but also the presence—even if no longer material—of many of history's notables. Named for Père de la Chaise—Louis XIV's confessor—the site was at one time occupied by a complex built to house members of the Jesuit religious order. In 1803, the land was purchased by the city of Paris, on order of Napoleon I, for development of the cemetery. Having expanded several times since its inception, Père Lachaise is Paris' largest cemetery.

Marcel Proust, born in 1871, succumbed to a final attack of asthma on November 18, 1922, at bed in his cork-lined room, surrounded by the manuscript that he continued to edit until the moment of his death. His grave, with its unassuming marker of black marble, lies in Section 85 of Père Lachaise within the family burial plot, built to honor the career of his physician father, Adrien Proust.

The Grave of Marcel Proust

Lachaise. On hearing about de Langlade, the Jim Morrison fan remarks, "it's a little spooky, isn't it?"

Proust's grave is an elegant slab of black marble. A few red roses have been strewn on top. The names of his family members are engraved on the sides of the marble stone. According to the map, the grave of Reynaldo Hahn, Proust's friend and lover, is nearby. We look but can't locate it. We look for a few other graves before Père Lachaise closes. We find those of Honoré de Balzac, Eugène Delacroix, Edith Piaf, Colette, Jim Morrison, Oscar Wilde, Gertrude Stein, and Frédéric Chopin.

The walk back is a little easier. It's downhill. We stop on the way at the Bistro Romain for dinner. It's a pleasant, but quick, meal because we're going to hear Vivaldi tonight—*Les Quatres Saisons (The Four Seasons)*—at the Sainte-Chapelle. Robin tries again to reach Marie and Brigitte before the concert begins. No luck.

We enter a gate of the Palais de Justice to get to the Sainte-Chapelle. This route leads directly to the upper church, formerly used by the royalty. We purchase our tickets and wait to be admitted. Finally, the crowd is allowed in. It's awe-inspiring . . . the walls look as though they're made entirely of stained glass. And even though it's almost dark, we can see that the colors in *les vitraux* (the stained glass windows), unlike in some of the other older structures, are brilliant.

There are eleven strings and a harpsichord in the ensemble. We hear Shubert, and then, Vivaldi's *Four Seasons*. The music is unbelievably beautiful. The audience is so pleased; they applaud for the solo violinist to be recalled twice and each time are rewarded with a bit more music. It's a cold, but short, walk back to the Ile Saint-Louis after the concert.

. . . the walls look as though they're made entirely of stained glass.

A few red roses . . .

The Sainte-Chapelle

Like a fugitive from the press of the Palais de Justice, the Sainte-Chapelle escapes upward, its high Gothic lines and lace-like spire stretching toward the heavens. The church—consecrated in 1248—was built as a reliquary to house sacred items, including the Crown of Thorns and fragments from the True Cross, purchased by King Louis IX from the Byzantine emperor.

Design of the Sainte-Chapelle is attributed to Pierre de Montreuil, though

uncertainty lingers regarding the identity of the church's architect. The structure consists of two levels: the lower chapel, used by the palace guards and those who served the royalty and the upper chapel—the private place of worship for the king and his family.

The interior of the upper chapel is dominated by 50-foot stained glass windows, most of which are original, thus representing the oldest and finest such collection in Paris. Just visible between the windows are *colonettes*—strands of stone—emphasizing the narrow verticality of the church and creating the illusion that the walls are made entirely of glass.

The Sainte-Chapelle withstood a fire in the seventeenth century and, like many structures associated with the royalty, it suffered some damage during the Revolution. Its relics were dispersed and for a time it was used as a warehouse to store flour. Efforts were undertaken during the nineteenth century to restore the church and today, as the windows refract the sunlight, one can hardly imagine—immersed in that chromatic reverie—that the Sainte-Chapelle was ever less than magnificent.

May 1

Labor Day

Today's the holiday—the French Labor Day. Robin has talked with Marie and Brigitte, so our visit to Saint-Étienne is on. We'll go there tomorrow; tonight we'll meet Brigitte and her boyfriend, Emmanuel, for dinner.

We know that, because of the holiday, we'll be limited to seeing attractions from the outside today. We walk across the courtyard of the Palais Royale, then on to Les Halles, Saint-Eustache, the Bourse de Commerce (the Commercial Exchange, and its birdcage), and the Pompidou Center. We conclude that the French expended all of their architectural creativity on the structures of antiquity. Their modern buildings are either sterile boxes or radical and weird. We stop for a bite to eat at a café near Les Halles; then, before the Pompidou, I buy a hat at an outdoor market.

The square in front of the Pompidou—a building turned inside out, which houses the National Gallery of Modern Art—is alive with activity. Spectators are gathered around a dancing troupe that's performing a tap routine to the music of Elvis Presley.

From the Pompidou we're on our way to the Place Vendôme, the Opéra, the Comédie Francaise, and the Madeleine. We stop briefly for a cup of coffee and a bathroom break, and I'm again challenged to decipher the locking, lighting, paying, timing, and positioning code for using French restrooms.

As we approach the Opéra, we see rows of police, with guns, in riot gear. I ask what's happening and an officer says that a *"petite manifestation"* (little demonstration) is taking place. With rows of police blocking the major streets, we're not at all convinced that it's so *"petite."* We get nearer and see red flags, with the Communist party insignia, blowing in the wind. The parade participants march to the accompaniment of French rap music. I buy some *muguets des*

For more than eight centuries, Les Halles was the central marketplace of Paris. Originally, a vast collection of open-air stands and stalls at which merchants hawked a variety of wares, the market gradually became populated primarily by vendors of food. It drew its name from *les halles*—the umbrella-like pavilions, built in the mid 1800s by Victor Balthard to enclose and protect the merchandise. Referred to as the "belly of Paris," Les Halles was so much more than a market; a public place where traders and buyers met, it reflected the vitality of the city—a point of confluence for the streams of human activity.

The late twentieth century saw the relocation of the market— compelled by population growth and congestion—to the Parisian suburb of Rungis. Today in place of the old market is the Forum des Halles—a huge, underground shopping and entertainment center and subway station, identifiable by tubular structures that seem to emerge on the surface like glass bubbles blown from below.

In contrast to the very modern appearance of the new marketplace, there stands—overlooking what was once the northwestern edge of Les Halles—a striking representative of the Middle Ages, the church of Saint-Eustache. Named for the second-century Roman general who converted to Christianity, Saint-Eustache started as a Gothic structure whose facade was later rebuilt in the style of the Renaissance. The building was constructed between 1532 and 1637.

Having served as the parish church for the merchants of Les Halles, Saint-Eustache was temporarily repurposed as the Temple of Agriculture during the Revolution. In 1844, it was damaged by fire but was later restored by Balthard.

Saint-Eustache is noted for its liturgical music and performances by famous composer/musicians, among whom numbered Liszt, Berlioz, and Verdi. Today, before the south front of the church, are displays of modern art. The most notable—l'Écoute—a giant, sculpted head with a hand cupped to one ear listens. . . for what? the bustle of the old market?

Carousel at Les Halles

L'Écoute at Saint-Eustache

Inaugurated in 1977, the Pompidou National Art and Cultural Center withstood a wave of negative reaction, following its debut, to become the biggest tourist attraction in Paris, drawing approximately eight million visitors each year. The center, which resembles a brightly colored oil refinery, is named for Georges Pompidou, president of France from 1969 to 1974 and modern art enthusiast. Construction of the Pompidou Center, also called the Beaubourg, was undertaken as a planned redevelopment of the area south of the former Les Halles market, which had been allowed to deteriorate.

The high-tech design of architects Renzo Piano and Richard Rogers places the structure's functional elements on its exterior, leaving the entire inner area free for display. The center contains the National Museum of Modern Art—which houses the works of all the major artists of the twentieth century, the Industrial Design Center, the Institute for Acoustic and Musical Research, a public library, and a film archive. The square to the west of the Pompidou serves as an open-air theater for all manner of street performers.

The Georges Pompidou National Art and Cultural Center

bois (lilies of the valley).

We stop at the Madeleine for a look and a rest. It's far more beautiful than I expected from its exterior. We get our tickets at the Gare Saint-Lazare for Saint-Étienne and head off to meet Brigitte.

Chez Paul is a small, intimate café off the Rue Faubourg Saint-Antoine, on the Rue Charonne. We're told it's very popular now because, apparently, it's the height of chic to be seen in a simple café. Brigitte and Emmanuel greet us at the door and we move to a table nearby. We converse in a mixture of French and English. Robin and Brigitte are catching up after twelve years of not seeing one another. Emmanuel's English is good; he can communicate the subtleties of humor. We have a long visit and agree to see them again for dinner at their apartment. They walk us back to the hotel.

May 2

Saint-Étienne

We have a wake-up call this morning. We're

. . . the height of chic to be seen in a simple café.

taking the metro to the Gare Montparnasse, where we'll get the TGV (*traine à grande vitesse,* i.e., bullet train) to Saint-Étienne. The train leaves at 7:01 A.M., so shortly after 6 A.M., we're walking down streets on which no one has yet begun to stir. We're able to board the train as soon as we arrive at the station. It has *un wagon-restaurant,* so we have breakfast on board. The train is comfortable and, although traveling at about 180 miles an hour, it's as smooth as silk. We soon fall asleep.

I wake up to see farmland and foothills whizzing by. Saint-Étienne is at the edge of Le Massif Central, a huge plateau in central France. Rain is streaming down the windows as we approach Lyons. We stop at the Lyons Par Dieu station. From the station, the city looks drably industrial and it, too, is hidden under a layer of graffiti. Waiting for the train to depart, I'm reminded that Lyons is a sister city of Saint Louis.

Rain is streaming . . .

From the Place de la Concorde one can see—between and behind the Ministry of Naval Affairs and the Hôtel Crillon—the Corinthian columns of the Church of St. Mary Magdalene (la Madeleine), its seeming reticence due, perhaps, to its unreligious appearance and a confused identity. Throughout the course of its existence, la Madeleine has been considered for use as a bank, a stock exchange, a railway station, and a theater.

Construction of the church, based on a design that sought to imitate the structure of Saint-Louis of the Invalids, began in 1764 during the reign of Louis XV. With the death in 1777 of the architect Constant d'Ivry, a new plan was forwarded to develop the church along the lines of the Panthéon. Building came to a halt under the Revolutionary government, as several different uses for the structure were considered. With the military successes of Napoleon came the decision to add la Madeleine to the list of monuments built to honor the army. Finally, Louis XVIII ordered that the edifice would be a place of worship. In 1975, the Church of St. Mary Magdalene was the site of the greatest state funeral ever held in honor of an American—that of the entertainer, Legion of Honor member, and French Resistance hero, Josephine Baker.

The Church of St. Mary Magdalene

The City of Lyons is a thriving metropolis, the capital of the Rhône department, at the confluence of the Rhône and Saône rivers, in east central France. The country's second most populated city, Lyons is home to approximately a half million residents. It is an economic and industrial center—a leader in the banking, pharmaceutical, printing, machine, and textile trades. The city is also recognized for several fine museums, historic buildings, a university, its futuristic opera house, and its cuisine.

Founded by Julius Caesar in 43 B.C. as the city of Lugdunum, Lyons became the capital of the Roman province of Gaul—evidenced by the remains of two Roman amphitheaters in which performances continue to be held.

The City of Lyons

Marie is at the station in Saint-Étienne to meet us. She is a stockier version of Brigitte, with dark, curly hair. We drive to the clothing store that she and Brigitte have opened. It's Marie's turn to tend the business while Brigitte, the clothing buyer, is in Paris. The store is called Lisa Calvo and is in the center of Saint-Étienne's pedestrian walk. Marie talks about what's happened in her life over the last twelve years. We'll meet her friend and ex-husband, Frédéric, for lunch. Meanwhile the rain prevents us from exploring the town, so we help out in the store, making suggestions to customers as they shop for clothing.

Frédéric arrives and we leave for a nearby Turkish restaurant. Robin and I have spicy eggplant and rice, while the proprietor tells us about his home, Turkey. We finish the meal with a demitasse of strong, Turkish coffee.

After lunch, we make a brief stop at Marie's apartment, a lovely place, with giant windows. Then back to the store. It's still raining, but Robin and I do

. . . so we help out in the store . . .

venture out on foot to the Monoprix, the *pharmacie* (I'm getting a cold), and the Nouvelle Galerie. Before long, Frédéric returns to the shop to take us to the station for our 6:00 P.M. train. We miss seeing Marie's mother and children. The sun comes out as we approach Paris. Back at the station, we get the metro to the Châtelet. Dinner, *poulet rôti and pommes frites* —my new favorite meal— is at Le Mistral.

May 3

A Last Look Around, A Final Meal with Friends

Tomorrow we leave. We can't believe the time has passed so quickly. We say we'll take it slow today, but I know we'll go for broke to get in as many more sights as possible. We walk to the Orangerie and are somewhat disappointed by the limited collection of Impressionists there, though the waterlilies of Monet make the visit worthwhile. Next, we walk inside the Petit Palais with its incredible entry foyer, and across the street to the Grand Palais—both built

Tomorrow we leave.

The Grand Palais was built during the years from 1897 to 1900 for the Universal Exposition of Paris. According to the inscription on its pediment, the conservatory was dedicated to "the glory of French art." The stone, steel, and glass structure is the work of architects Deglane, Louvet, and Thomas. In 1964, French Minister of Art André Malraux transformed a portion of the Grand Palais to accommodate temporary exhibits. In addition to art exhibitions, the 54,000 square foot space of the Grand Palais also has housed large commercial displays such as auto and home shows.

The Grand Palais

Just across the Avenue Winston Churchill from the Grand Palais sits the Petit Palais. Constructed at the same time as its larger neighbor, the Petit Palais—now home to the Museum of Fine Arts of the City of Paris—was used during the 1900 Exposition to present a retrospective of French art. The monument was designed in the grand and decorative style of the architect Charles Girault and required, for its completion, the work of thirteen sculptors. Today, the Petit Palais contains an assortment of art collections.

for the Universal Exhibition in 1900. The Grand Palais is a huge art nouveau convention center. We thought the Toulouse Lautrec exhibit was on display here, but inside there are no signs of it.

We begin our trek to the Bois de Boulogne. This is a 2000-plus acre park with recreations of every sort. En route, we have our best opportunity to see the ornate Pont Alexandre. We stop nearby for a quick lunch. In the Bois, we walk around the entire Lac Inférieur. There are two islands in the lake and we imagine that the restaurant visible from the shore must be the one in which Proust's character, Marcel, was stood up by one of his many loves. After circling the lake, we decide we'd better get over to the Bat-O-Bus so we'll get to Brigitte's on time.

Patricia has told us that we must buy the boat tickets at the Pont d'Alma. We make a mad dash there, only to find out that that is the point of departure for the *bateaux mouches*, from which we can not

We run out and hop onto the boat just minutes before it's scheduled to leave.

disembark at the Hôtel de Ville. We're afraid we've missed the last Bat-O-Bus, but go there anyway and are delighted to find that we can still board the last one. Robin and I get on what we think is the boat. How nice it is! Two levels, bathrooms, a concession stand. We walk to what looks like the deck and fortunately discover, before the real boat pulls off, that we're still on the pier. We run out and hop onto the boat just minutes before it's scheduled to leave. The ride along the Seine is relaxing. We see the now familiar landmarks from a different perspective, and this last look seems a fitting close to our visit.

Getting off at the Hôtel de Ville, we hurry into the metro and arrive at Brigitte and Manuel's by 8:00 P.M. They've prepared a wonderful meal, of many courses, as is the French tradition: avocado with caviar, *pommes dauphinois*, fish, *fromage*, and dessert. Their apartment is small and they can't afford such an expensive spread, but they've obviously put in a spein Paris, the Pont Alexandre III is certainly the most flamboyant. Designed by the architects Resal and Alby, the bridge was built—together with the Grand Palais and the Petit Palais—for the Universal Exposition of 1900. It commemorates the Franco-Russian alliance of 1892 and, thus, was named for Czar Alexander III of Russia (1845-1894), whose son—Czar Nicholas II—laid its foundation stone in 1896. Construction of the single-span Alexandre III Bridge was completed within two years.

Adorned with gilded sculptures along its length and lit by lampposts with globes of handblown glass, the Pont Alexandre III is a fitting representative of the gaity and enthusiasm of the Belle Époque. Its axis is coincident with the esplanade of the Hôtel des Invalides on the Left Bank and extends, at the opposite end, between the Grand Palais and Petit Palais.

The Pont Alexandre III

The *bateaux mouches* and the *bateaux vedettes* are large excursion boats that glide along the Seine, providing visitors with stunning views of the city's highlights. Typically, audio commentary—in any one of several languages—can be heard as the boats drift past the major landmarks. The shuttle boats depart for what, usually, are hour-long tours from a number of locations, including the Pont d'Iéna, the Pont Neuf, and the Pont de l'Alma. The boat excursions are especially dramatic at night when the monuments are illuminated.

Shuttle Boats on the Seine

cial effort. We talk about books—Emmanuel asks us to send him some works by Jack Kerouac—music, and cultural differences. They say that in France, one usually dines with friends about twice a week. A nice custom. I leave my address with Brigitte. We all say goodbye. Robin and I walk back to the hotel, pay our bill, and ask for a taxi for tomorrow morning.

One last croissant and café au lait.

May 4

Heading Home

We drop our luggage off in the entrance foyer and I tell Patricia we'll be having breakfast downstairs in case the taxi comes. She refuses to charge us for breakfast. One last croissant and café au lait. The taxi is here. Patricia asks us to send her a postcard. We're headed home.

A nice custom.

Index

Index

Index

Index

DÉJEUNERS,
GOÛTERS,
COLLATIONS,
BRUNCHES.

№ 000242

SNCF

PARIS MONTPARNASSE

ILLIERS COMBRAY

valable DU 28.04.92 AU 27.06.92

POUR L'ALLER ET LE RETOUR

Particularités

EURYDICE

10, Place des Vosges
75004 Paris
Tél.: 42.77.77.99

28419

MUSÉES NATIONAUX

ENTRÉE

TARIF RÉDUIT
16 F

8419

ICE, INC.
MISSOURI 63109

004 Paris

*113/*114
56   010105
RIS AUST
.04.92
1.736010

2976362

ENTREE MUSEE

PT 26-04

Réunion des

LOUVR

(2)

BAR   21   Eaux minérales

22   Alcools, Liqueurs
spiritueux

23   Autres bo

Liqueurs, spiritueux

, bière